The book

The recipes in this book were given to me by some people I was fortunate enough to meet. These people were a colourful mix of black Africans, Asians, Caribbeans, Indonesians, South Americans, Canadians and Europeans. They all have one thing in common - they are passionate about saving animals from extinction. This is why they had come to the tiny island of Jersey to study conservation and management of endangered species at the Durrell Wildlife Conservation Trust.

Whilst they were studying, I cooked for them. It was part of my role as housekeeper of the International Training Centre. In the cosy dining room, students from all over the world would get to know each other and exchange ideas. People also liked to hang out in the kitchen, attracted by the gorgeous smells, and if I was lucky, they might even cook a dish from their home cuisine to share with their fellow students.

Anna with some students i

Anna Wimberley

Durrell

Durrell Wildlife Conservation Trust is an international charity working globally towards our mission of saving species from extinction. Founded in 1959 Durrell has built up a worldwide reputation for its pioneering conservation techniques, developed under the leadership of its founder, the late renowned author and naturalist Gerald Durrell.

Working with a wide range of international partners, we combine the skills of our staff at our wildlife park, our field programmes and our training programmes to save some of the most threatened species in the most threatened places.

Headquartered in Jersey, the International Training Centre also supports the development of future conservationists and has educated nearly 3,000 graduates from around 128 countries.

Sumatran orangutan, Pongo abelii

Snacks

Cheese Bread	06
Potato and Carrot Tart	08
Potato Croquettes	10
Chapatti	12
Chapatti Wrap	14
Spicy Potatoes	16

Fish

Fish Curry	20
Fish Stew	22
Imperial Rice with Seafood	24
Pickled Vegetable with Fried Fish	26
Peanut Butter Fish	28

Chicken

Chicken Adobo	32
Chicken Pelau	34
Steamed Chicken	36
Chicken Stew	38
Chicken Tapas	40

Meat

Big Pot	44
Steamed Mutton with Rice	46
Beef Stew	48
Meat Pie	50
Beef and Sweet Greens	52
Jollof Rice	54

Veggie

Egg Pasties	58
Thick Lentil Soup	60
Pasta Cheese Casserole	62
Bean Stew	64
Brocco Bella Lasagne	66
Cornmeal Coo Coo	68

Sweet

Rice Pudding	72
Sweet Potato Pudding	74
Spiced Honey Cake	76
Banana Bread	78
Apricot Tart	80

Fish

Fish Curry | Sri Lanka

Serves 4

- 500g fish, chopped into pieces
- 1 tsp. curry powder
- 1 tsp. chili powder
- 1 tsp. turmeric powder
- 2 tbsp. lime juice
- 2 bell peppers, diced
- 1 garlic clove, chopped
- 1 tsp. finely chopped ginger
- 1 ripe tomato, chopped
- 2 tbsp. oil
- 1 big onion
- 2 cups(340ml) coconut milk
- 1 green chili, de-seeded and chopped small
- salt

How to make:

Rub the fish all over with salt, curry powder, chili powder and turmeric. Squeeze some lime juice over the fish and marinate for 15 minutes.

In some oil, fry the ginger, garlic, and then onion, bell peppers, tomato and green chili. Fry gently for 5-10 minutes. Turn heat down to very low, add the pieces of fish and simmer for 5 minutes.

Last of all add the coconut milk. Stir. Simmer for 15-20 minutes.

Put the lid on the pan and let it rest for a while.

This curry should be served with plain rice.

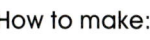

'Curry' means sauce. It is made with different spices sometimes sold as curry powder. These include cumin, cloves, coriander, cardamom, cinnamon, many of them originally from Sri Lanka.

Deepani with a youngster at the Elephant Rehabilitation Centre

Deepani Jayantha from Sri Lanka studied Veterinary Medicine at Colombo. Her first work placement was at the Udawalawa Elephant Transit Home. This government-run institution takes care of young orphaned elephants and gives them shelter, food and medical attention, until they are old enough to lead an independent life. As Deepani's interest in elephants grew, she took on the task of following them as they were released into the bush, monitoring their progress, as they joined groups of wild elephants.

Sri Lankan elephant *Elephas maximus* [EN]

Fish Stew | Philippines
Kare Kare

Serves 4

- 500g fish fillet
- ½ tsp. ginger juice
- 3 tbsp. cornflour
- 5 cloves garlic, chopped small
- 1 onion
- 1 beef stock cube
- 4 runner beans, cut into pieces
- 1 banana bud, trimmed and sliced
- 1 aubergine, sliced
- tbsp. achuete juice
- 3 chopped tomatoes
- tbsp. rice flour
- 3 tbsp. roasted peanuts, pounded
- salt, pepper and oil

How to make:

Sprinkle fish with ginger juice. Season with salt and pepper. Let it marinate for a few minutes. Coat each portion of fish in cornflour and fry gently until brown. Set aside.

In a pan sauté the chopped onion and garlic. Make up the bouillon with boiling water. Add this together with all the vegetables and achuete juice.

Simmer for 20 mins. or until vegetables are cooked.

Add the fish and cook for a few minutes more. Thicken with ground peanuts and rice flour.

Serve with bagoong (fermented fish paste).

Fish sauce (or fish paste) goes with nearly all Filipino dishes. It is a condiment made with fish that has been allowed to ferment. To westerners it may smell revolting, but to Filippinos it is the final touch to a good meal.

crocodile growing tanks

Jude Dimalibot from the Philippines worked for the local government on Palawan Island. As a staff member of the Environmental Research Unit, one of her tasks was to develop management strategies for endangered species on the island. The Palawan Wildlife and Rescue Center, formerly called The Crocodile Farm, has become one of the island's biggest assets, both for conservation and for the tourism industry. It includes a crocodile clinic and a breeding station for the endangered Philippines crocodile *Crocodylus mindorensis* [CR].

Jude Dimalibot

Imperial Rice with Seafood | Cuba

Serves 4

- 500g cooked seafood
- 1 tbsp. vegetable oil
- 8 tomatoes, chopped
- 1 onion, chopped
- 2 cloves garlic, crushed
- 1 red or green pepper
- salt and pepper
- 300g rice
- 50g mayonnaise
- 50g grated cheese
- 1 tsp. turmeric
- 800ml fish stock

How to make:

Fry chopped onion, garlic and tomatoes, and cook with strips of pepper until soft.

Mix the cooked seafood with the tomato sauce.

In a separate pan, cook the rinsed rice in the fish stock with the turmeric.

When the rice is fluffy layer ingredients in an ovenproof dish – a third of the rice first, followed by half the seafood in sauce, then a third of the rice, the mayonnaise, the rest of the seafood in sauce then the final third of rice followed by the cheese. The top layer must be cheese. Put in the oven and bake until the cheese is melted.

The term seafood refers to edible saltwater fish and shellfish. There are two main types of shellfish, those with jointed shells (crabs, lobsters, prawns) and molluscs (mussels, oysters, scallops). Shellfish should be bought fresh on the day they are going to be cooked as they do not keep.

Cuban green-headed anole

Alicia Perez Angel from Cuba has been studying Cuban lizards, especially the endangered anolis [DD] species. The Cuban green anole *Anolis porcatus* is fascinating to watch: It changes colour, from brown when it is resting, to green when it is active.

Alicia Perez Angel

Taking part in the Durrell Endangered Species Management Graduate Certificate Course in Jersey in 2005 has helped Alicia design a diet and feeding program for these lizards. The aim is to breed them in the National Zoo, and if successful, replenish the dwindling population in the wild.

Pickled Vegetable with Fried Fish | China

Serves 4

- 400g pickled vegetables
- 600g fish or fish fillet
- 1 tomato
- 1 red chili
- 3 tsp brown sugar
- salt
- add oil and butter for frying

How to make:

Cut the fish into chunks and fry on both sides in a little oil and butter. Set aside.

Cut the tomato into slices and the chili into strips, then stir-fry all the vegetables together with some of the juice from the pickled vegetables.

Pour some water into the fried vegetables and add sugar and salt for seasoning. Simmer until it turns into a sauce.

Lay the fried fish on top and simmer for another three minutes.

For pickled vegetables you can soak any of your favourite vegetables (peppers/onions/cucumber) in wine-vinegar for at least 3 days. Alternatively you can buy it from a shop.

Victoria crowned pigeon - New Guinea

Lai Yuk-Ming from China is a bird keeper at Hong Kong Zoological and Botanical Gardens. This is a place where people come to relax and unwind after a hard day at work.

Lai Yuk-Ming

Here Lai Yuk-Ming is seen holding a Victoria crowned pigeon *Goura victoria* [VU]. These beautiful birds have suffered rapid population declines in the wild, as a result of habitat destruction and hunting. They are hunted for their meat as well as for their beautiful feathers. The fact that they fly onto low perches when threatened, makes them easy targets in all populated areas.

Peanut Butter Fish | Sierra Leone
Granat Soup

Serves 4

- ½ jar salted peanut butter
- 1 red chili
- 500g white fish
- 1 onion, chopped small
- 2 cloves garlic
- 2 cm fresh ginger
- 6 tomatoes
- 1 tbsp. tomato puree
- cooking oil
- 240ml of water
- 1 lemon juiced (optional)

How to make:

Cut the fish into portions, season with salt and marinate with lemon (optional).

In a saucepan gently fry the onion with diced garlic and chopped ginger.

Add the diced chili, the chopped tomatoes and a splash of water, and simmer for 15-20 minutes. In a bowl or jug combine the tomato puree with the water and peanut butter. Stir well until it becomes a thin smooth paste and add to the saucepan.

Stir in well and cook for another 10-15 minutes. Meanwhile, fry fish briefly then add to saucepan and cook with the sauce for last 5 minutes. Serve with rice.

Dorado a fish similar to seabass, is commonly eaten in Sierra Leone, often grilled whole or in equal sized pieces. Peanut sauce, made with cayenne, chili and garlic, is nearly always used as dressing for this kind of fish.

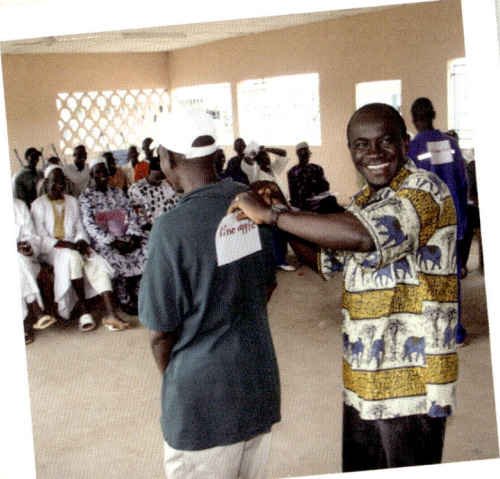

Torjia organising an education game at a community enterprise workshop

Torjia Karimu works as a Chimpanzee Conservation Manager and general Conservation Planner in Sierra Leone. In November 2005 a project was set up, led by the Jane Goodall Institute, to establish a strategy relating to chimpanzee protection and conservation in Sierra Leone and Guinea. Torjia Karimu was the manager and coordinator of the Sierra Leone team, liaising with all the stakeholders and monitoring the fieldwork and overall progress. Although the funding ended in August 2007, he carried on, with some of the staff.

Common chimpanzee *Pan troglodytes* [EN].

Chicken

Chicken Adobo | The Philippines

Serves 4

- 1 chicken, cut in pieces
- ½ head garlic, crushed
- 120ml vinegar
- 3 tbsp. soy sauce
- 240ml water
- 6 peppercorns
- 480ml thick coconut milk (optional)

How to make:

Combine the garlic with the vinegar and soy sauce and marinate the chicken pieces, turning a few times.

Add water and peppercorns and bring to the boil. Simmer until chicken is tender.

Add coconut milk and cook for a few minutes more.

For ordinary adobo, omit coconut milk.

Serve with rice.

Some people sear the chicken pieces in oil, before they cook them. You get that lovely caramelized taste, together with the sweet and sour.

Joanne examining a macaque

Joanne Justo from the Philippines has been a vet at the Palawan Wildlife and Rescue Centre since 2002. Although a sanctuary for many of Palawan's endemic animals, it is still most famous for its crocodiles. Many visitors come throughout the year, and to actually hold a baby croc may be one of the highlights of their holiday.

Photo (left): The macaque has been sedated and Joanne is looking for the vein in order to take some blood. The Philippine long-tailed macaque *Macaca fascicularis philippinenesis* [NT] is the only primate species (besides humans!) native to Palawan.

Philippine Long-tailed macaque

Chicken Pelau | St. Vincent and the Grenadines

Serves 4

- 1 chicken
- 2 tbsp oil
- 1 tbsp. brown sugar
- 300g rice
- 125g dry lentils, add cooked according to instructions on packet
- salt
- pepper
- 1 onion

How to make:

Cut the chicken into pieces, take off the skin and remove the bigger bones. Season.

Heat the oil in a big pot, add the sugar and allow it to caramelize.

Put the seasoned meat into the pot and stir until well covered in burnt sugar. Add rice into the pot and cook with the chicken for a few minutes.

Now the chopped onion goes in together with the cooked lentils. Season to taste and cover with water.

Turn down the heat, cover and simmer, topping up with water ever so often, until all the water has evaporated and the rice is soft.

Seasoning the chicken doesn't just mean sprinkle with salt and pepper. You have to marinate it for several hours in a mixture of chopped onion, garlic and soy sauce, turning the meat a few times.

Looking at you from this photo is a St. Vincent parrot

Bradford Latham, from the Forestry Department of the Caribbean Islands of St. Vincent and the Grenadines, has been assessing and monitoring the wild population of the St. Vincent parrot *Amazona guildingii* [VU] as well as establishing a genetically sound breeding programme at the Nicholls Wildlife Complex. Even though the St Vincent parrot has been declared the National Bird and has in fact been protected since 1987, people still hunt this bird.

"Parrots are intelligent animals that need a lot of interaction and stimulation. If these are not met, they will show signs of abnormal behaviour like screaming, aggression, extreme fearlessness and feather plucking."

Bradford Latham 2005

Bradford Latham

Steamed Chicken | China

Serves 4

- 1 whole fresh chicken
- 4 cloves shallots
- 2 spring onions
- 40g root ginger
- 1 tsp. salt
- 2 tbsp. Chinese rice wine
- 2 tbsp. light soy sauce

How to make:

Clean the chicken and dry with a towel.

Rub the chicken skin and cavity with salt and rice wine. Marinate for at least 30 minutes.

Stuff ginger and spring onions into the cavity. Steam the chicken in a pot with tight fitting lid. Allow 20 minutes per 500g.

Chop the shallots and fry in a saucepan. Mix with light soy sauce and the liquid from the steamed chicken.

Serve with rice.

If you prefer a dark colour chicken you can boil it in a mixture of 2 tsp. dark sugar, 250ml dark soy sauce and 300ml water, turning frequently. Serve with the gravy.

orangutans at Durrell's outside enclosure

Chik Suet-Ha from China works at the Hong Kong Zoo and Botanical Gardens. She is responsible for the facilities and staff management of the Gardens. She came to take part in the Durrell Endangered Species Management Graduate Certificate Course in 2005.

Chik Suet-Ha

Whilst she was studying for the Durrell Endangered Species Management Graduate Certificate Course in Jersey, she drew up plans for an enclosure for orangutans at Hong Kong Zoo.

The picture was taken at the Jersey outdoor enclosure for Sumatran orangutans *Pongo abelii* [CR] and shows the sixteen year old Mawar with her son Gempa who is holding on for dear life, he is only a few weeks old.

Chicken Stew | Tanzania
Wali Kuku

Serves 4

- 4 chicken portions
- small piece of ginger, finely chopped
- 1-2 onions, peeled and chopped
- 6 tomatoes, diced
- 4 Irish potatoes, peeled and chopped
- 2 garlic cloves, peeled and crushed
- salt and pepper
- 1 tsp. cumin
- oil
- 4 handfuls of rice

How to make:

Chop the onion and fry in a big pot for one or two minutes.

Crush the garlic and chop the ginger into small pieces, then add these together with some cumin to the onions. Give it a stir.

Add the chicken, potato and tomato and cook for another 5 minutes. Top up with water until just covered and simmer until the chicken is done.

Serve with rice.

With mainland Tanzania producing rice(Wali) and chicken(Kuku) and Zanzibar supplying many spices, a great variety of Wali Kuku can be found, some hot, some spicy, some curried.

Ali with President of Zanzibar

Ali Said Hamad from Tanzania has taken on the huge task of establishing a marine life protected area, in the Pemba Channel between the islands of Zanzibar and the Tanzanian mainland. An information centre has been set up on the small island of Misali.

The picture shows the president of Zanzibar, His Excellency Aman A. Karume and his entourage on a visit to Misali Island. Ali is showing them round.

The government in Zanzibar takes the conservation of its valuable coastal resources very seriously, recently banning the importation of plastic bags, to save turtles who would otherwise become tangled with plastic floating in the sea.

Chicken Tapas | Colombia
Ajiaco

Serves 4

- 500g potatoes
- 1 tin sweetcorn
- 500g chicken breast
- 1 avocado
- 1 tsp. of capers
- 80ml single cream
- rice

How to make:

Cook the chicken with the potatoes in water until they almost dissolve (at least 1 hour), then season to your liking.

Cut the chicken breast into thin slices.

In a dish mix the sweetcorn with the cream and a teaspoonful of capers. Put slices of chicken breast on top.

In another dish serve some rice decorated with slices of avocado.

Place the potato mixture into a bed for the chicken to be served on.

Ajiaco is very versatile. You may use other kinds of meat like pork and beef, maybe marinate them before cooking with the potatoes. Add extra vegetables like plantain, pumpkin or sweet potato.

The main thing is to cook it for at least an hour.

Honey harvesting using a branch of a tree to anchor a hive

Isadora Martinez

Isadora Martinez from Colombia has been joint project manager of ACCB (Angkor Centre for Conservation and Biodiversity) in Cambodia.

To promote understanding of environmental issues, a mobile unit has been set up to give lectures and organise activities for local communities.

The aim is to develop sustainable use of natural resources. One example of this is ACCBee, a project training local people in beekeeping and honey extraction.

meat

Big Pot | Poland
Bigos

Serves 8-10

- ½ kg of sauerkraut
- ¼ kg of white cabbage
- ½ kg of beef (stewing or braising)
- ¼ kg of pork shoulder
- ¼ kg of smoked bacon
- 5 dried plums
- 6 dried mushrooms
- 6 bay leaves
- 5-6 peppercorns
- 5-6 pimento seeds
- 1 tbsp. salt

How to make:

Put the beef and shoulder of pork into a heat-proof dish. Pour water into it to make the meat soft and juicy. Pre-heat the oven to 150°C and bake the meat for about 2 hours.

Take it out onto a board, but keep the stock. Cut the meat into medium size cubes. Cut the smoked bacon into small pieces. Slice fresh white cabbage and mix with sauerkraut and the cut meat.

Pour the stock over it and mix well. Add a little salt, mushrooms, plums, peppercorns, pimento seeds, bay leaves and any spices you like. Cook everything together for a further hour.

This recipe is changing with time, some people add red wine, some add tomatoes or fresh green peppers. In the past people used wild pig's meat. But remember: most important is good quality sauerkraut!

Fire salamander

Agnieszka Ogrodowczyk from Poland came to Jersey in 2001 to participate in the Durrell Endangered Species Management Graduate Certificate Course. It was the beginning of an amazing career.

In cooperation with Durrell, she joined the conservation team in St. Lucia, counting, recording, observing and monitoring the St. Lucia whiptail *Cnemidophorus vanzoi* [VU].

After two years of fieldwork and a brief spell at Durrell, she returned to her native Poland to study for a PhD. Her subject is the fire salamander *Salamandra salamandra* [LC].

"I have worked in zoos, then I did fieldwork in the Caribbean, still something seemed to be missing. What was it? I went back to do research for my PhD. Now I have all the pieces together: science, working with animals and conservation." **Agnes**

Agnieszka Ogrodowczyk

Steamed Mutton with Rice | China

Serves 4

- 5 carrots, chopped into chunks
- 190g rice
- 1 onion, cut up small
- 1 kg mutton, cut into small pieces
- 100 ml vegetable oil
- 1 tsp. cumin (seeds or powder)
- salt

How to make:

Cut the carrots and the mutton into chunks, dice the onion very small.

Heat up half the oil in a wok, sprinkle in some cumin. Fry the meat with the onions and put aside in a separate dish. In the same wok, gently fry the carrots until soft in the remainder of the oil.

Leave half of the carrots at the bottom, put the meat and onion on top, then ladle on the other half of the carrots, then the rice. Add some water and bring to the boil. Turn down the heat and put a tight lid on. Always keep the rice moist, either by adding water or turning it over in spoonfuls. When the rice has become sticky, mix everything completely.

How do you know when to add water to the rice? If you listen to the noise the rice makes, you can tell whether it still needs water adding. Hissing and crackling means it is getting dry, bubbling means it is too wet.

Chinese stripe-necked turtle

Dr. Shi Haitao from China teaches ecology, zoology and wildlife management at Hainan University. His research into turtle farming led him to develop an action plan for turtle conservation in China following the course Durrell Endangered Species Management Graduate Certificate Course 2003, he took at Durrell.

Dr. Shi Haitao

Turtles are being bred and sold in China on a massive scale. The demand is there, because they are the main ingredient for 'turtle soup', they are also used in traditional Chinese medicine. Originally taken from the wild, they are being bred and inter-bred on turtle farms, for sale in China as well as for export. Now more than 50% of freshwater turtles are regarded as endangered or critically endangered. Chinese stripe-necked turtle *Mauremys sinensis* [EN].

Beef Stew | Philippines
Niligang Baka

Serves 4

- 1 kg beef (for stewing) cut into chunk cubes
- 4 small onions
- ½ head garlic
- 2 tbsp oil
- pinch of salt and pepper
- 7 medium potatoes
- 3 carrots (optional)
- 10 leaves of cabbage
- 12 pieces bok choy
- 2 tbsp. fish sauce
- 2 tbsp. vegetable oil

How to make:

To prepare, cut each cabbage leaf into four, the same with the pieces of bok choy and the carrots.

Dice the onions and crush the garlic. In a soup pot, brown the onion and garlic in the oil. Add the beef and water, bring to boil, lower the heat and let simmer for about an hour or two, until the beef is tender.

Remove the scum that will rise to the top of the pot and keep the stock clear.

Cut the potatoes into cubes and add to the stew. Bring up to a boil to cook the potatoes. Lower heat and put in the vegetables. Cook uncovered for 20 minutes. Season with salt, pepper and fish sauce.

Fish sauce in Filipino cooking is a must. Maybe you cannot get hold of it. Never mind: it will taste nice just with a few squirts of soy sauce added as a finishing touch.

Philippine Tarsier – an endangered Tarsier species endemic to the Philippines

Emilia Lastica

Emilia Lastica trained to be a vet in the Philippines. She then joined the Negros Forest Ecological Foundation's biodiversity centre in 1999 and came to Jersey two years later to study with other students on the Durrell Endangered Species Management Graduate Certificate Course. Since then she has been a tireless advocate for threatened species. Emilia has taken on the challenging task of professionalising zookeeping in the Philippines, from breeding endangered species to wild animal management, medical practices, networking, education and training.

Philippine Tarsier *Tarsius syrichta* [NT].

Meat Pie | South Africa
Bobotie

Serves 4

- 2 medium onions
- 2 tbsp. fat (this can be butter, dripping or oil)
- 1 tbsp. curry powder
- 1 tbsp. sugar
- 1 tbsp. vinegar
- 100g raisins and dried apricots (optional)
- 500g raw minced pork or beef
- 1 thick slice of bread
- 300ml milk
- 2 eggs
- salt

How to make:

It helps to soak any dried fruit in water, to soften.

Fry the chopped-up onions until lightly browned. Sprinkle curry powder over. Add salt, sugar and vinegar.

Soak the bread in warm milk, drain off any excess milk and mash.

In a bowl mix together the meat, the fried onions, mushy bread, one beaten egg and any pre-soaked dried fruit.

Turn into a buttered oven proof dish. Beat the remaining egg with the rest of the milk, season with salt and pepper and pour over the meat.

Dot with small flecks of butter and cook in the oven at 180°C, for 30-40 minutes.

Bobotie is served with yellow rice. Sometimes raisins are added in with the rice. As this is a rich dish, a green salad with lettuce, tomatoes and parsley makes a perfect partner.

African wild dog - Eastern and Southern Africa

Tracy Rehse from South Africa works in the Research Department at Pretoria Zoo. She is responsible for developing a species management programme for the zoo, concentrating on the African wild dog *Lycaon pictus* [EN] and the Southern ground hornbill *Bucorvus cafer* [VU]. Her methods include studbook keeping, genetic analysis and small population management theory.

She also works with other zoos to set up and co-ordinate joint breeding and management strategies – cooperation is vital to the future survival of endangered species.

Tracy Rehse

9 weeks old

Beef and Sweet Greens | Madagascar
Henomby sy anamamy

Serves 4

- 1 kg stewing beef (or zebu)
- 2 cloves garlic
- 4 tomatoes
- 1 onion
- oil
- some greens (or spinach)
- 1 tbsp. salt
- water

How to make:

Cut the beef into chunks. Put them in a pot and cover with water. Simmer slowly for 1 ½ hours, topping up with water every now and then, to stop the meat getting dry.

Chop the tomatoes, slice the onions and crush the garlic. Stir them in with the beef and cook for another 30 minutes.

Wash the sweet greens and remove the hardest part. Put a little oil into a pot, add the greens with some water, simmer for 5 minutes. Stir and add some salt.

Serve the greens with the beef stew and rice.

When you cook rice in water, let it burn dry a little, then when you take out the rice, there is some stuck at the bottom of the pan. Let it burn a bit more until it gives off a lovely aroma. Pour some water on it and boil it until the water turns brown. This makes a tasty drink called Ranovola.

Jonah holding a wild black and white ruffed lemur

Jonah Ratsimbazafy from Madagascar has been studying the behaviour of the black and white ruffed lemurs *Varecia variegata variegata* [EN], especially in the Manombo rainforest. These graceful animals have become quite rare, because of illegal hunting, logging and slash-and-burn activities, to get more land for agriculture. This has reduced their habitat to a few fragments of forest along the coast.

Jonah is the coordinator of a project to save the biodiversity of plants and animals in the Manombo rainforest. On a village level this means talking with local people, who then form village associations, it means training some to study the lemurs, it means going into schools to get the message across to children, and collaborating with local and government authorities.
It's all connected.

Jollof Rice | Ghana
Benachin

Serves 4

- 500g braising steak
- water
- 2 onions
- oil
- 4 eggs
- 2 tbsp. tomato puree
- salt and pepper
- 500g rice

How to make:

Put meat in a pot and cover with water. Season with salt, add one diced onion and simmer for 20 minutes or until tender.

Drain the meat and fry it in oil. Take the meat out of the pan and set aside.

Boil the eggs and then fry in the same fat as the meat until they are brown. Set aside.

Cut up another onion and fry briefly, then add the tomato purée, the rice and 1½ litres of water.

When the rice is done, season with salt and pepper. Mix the meat and the eggs in with the rice.

Jollof Rice is eaten in many parts of West Africa. It is delicious and easy to prepare. The main ingredients are rice, tomatoes and onion. You can make it with beef or chicken and add spices, depending on what you've got in store. Jollof Rice is often served with fried plantains.

Diana monkey

Stephen Tamanja is a veterinary technician in Ghana. He left Accra Zoo in February 2007, along with all the animals, when it was closed down to make way for a new presidential complex. He is still studying the threats to wildlife in his country, and hopes to join a new conservation center that is taking shape in Achimota Forest, just outside Accra. Established by the Ghanaian Wildlife Commission together with the international organization WAPCA (West Africa Primates Conservation Action), the new Primate Centre already holds several critically endangered monkey species such as the white-naped mangabey *Cercocebus atys* [VU] and the Diana monkey *Cercopithecus diana* [VU]. Collaborating with 12 European zoos, the center will be an exciting new development for a country where monkeys are still considered a delicacy and hunted for bushmeat.

Stephen Tamanja

Veggie

Egg Pasties | Colombia
Arepa de hueva

Makes 4

- 5 ripe tomatoes, chopped
- 2 bunches of spring onions, finely chopped
- 6 garlic cloves, finely chopped
- 1/2 cup of chopped cilantro (coriander leaves)
- 1/4 cup of olive oil (60ml)
- salt and black pepper
- 160g harina (corn meal)
- 1/4 tsp. salt
- 1 1/4 cup boiling water (300ml)
- 4-5 eggs

How to make:

Make the filling – Sauté the first four ingredients in olive oil. Season and put aside.

Mix the harina and salt, then add hot water by the ladlefull, whilst stirring. When it becomes too thick to stir, use your hands to form a pliable mass.

When it is cool enough to handle, roll out 1cm thick between two clear plastic sheets. Cut rounds of 15cm diameter, fold over in half and carefully press the edges together.

Deep fry until puffed up, but still white. Now comes the difficult bit: lift out the pasty and make a hole in the side, slip in some filling followed by a raw egg. Seal the hole. A couple more minutes in the deepfryer, and it will be ready: hot, crunchy and golden brown.

If you want an easier version of Arepa, just leave out the eggs. Prepare a filling of your choice. This could be chicken, mushroom, in fact anything made into a mash with cooked potatoes and onion. Put a spoonful of this on each round, press together and deep-fry, once only!

White-footed tamarin

Ana Carolina from Colombia is working as the Chief Vet of Piscilago Zoo. In the last two years she has been focusing on three animals in particular: the rare Orinoco crocodile *Crocodylus intermedius* [CR], the Southern river otter *Lontra povocax* [EN] and the rare white-footed tamarin *Sanguinus leucopus* [EN]. She organised a workshop for veterinarians to study causes of mortality for white-footed tamarins in captivity, helping to maintain a captive breeding population of this beautiful endangered animal.

Ana Carolina

Southern river otter

Thick Lentil Soup | India
Dal

Serves 4

- 250g lentils
- 1 tsp. turmeric (optional)
- salt to taste
- 2-3 tbsp. of vegetable oil
- 1 onion, finely chopped
- 4 cloves garlic, grated
- 1 tbsp. coriander seeds
- 1 tbsp. cumin seeds
- 1 green chilli, minced
- 4 tomatoes, finely chopped
- 1 tsp. garam masala

How to make:

Soak the lentils overnight and cook in plenty of water. You can add a teaspoonful of turmeric and salt to the lentils whilst cooking.

In a separate pan, heat up the oil and fry the seeds gently, then add the chopped onion, garlic and chilli. Cook them till they are brown.

Add grated tomatoes and garam masala and cook till the oil separates.

Pour the lentils into this pan and cook for five minutes.

Garnish with green coriander leaves.

For a light lunch serve with Indian flat-breads such as Chapattis or Puris and a fresh salad.

Poorly leopard cub (nearly one and a half months old)

Sat Pal Dhiman is working as a range officer in Himachal Pradesh, Northern India. He is responsible for protecting wildlife in two reserves: Majathal and Darlaghat. Sometimes wild animals stray into areas of human habitation, like this leopard cub *Panthera pardus* [NR].

'This female leopard cub was nearly one and a half months old and was in a healthy condition. The mother was in fact around the village hiding in a patch of forest. The cub was released back into her mother's territory near the den and is being monitored by the field staff. We are hoping that mother will retrieve the cub.' Sat Pal

Sat Pal Dhiman

Pasta Cheese Casserole | Germany
Käsespätzle

Serves 4

Pasta:
- 250g plain flour
- 2 eggs
- ½ tsp. salt
- 150ml water

Casserole:
- strong-tasting cheese
- 1 medium onion
- butter

How to make:

Sieve flour into mixing bowl then add about ¾ of the egg and water mixture then add more liquid as required. Beat it with a wooden spoon until it comes away from the side of the bowl. Let it rest for a while.

Put plenty of water to boil in a very large pot. Add some salt. Then put a metal plate with holes (this could be a grater or a colander) over the top of the pot. Push the soft dough to and fro, so that it falls into the boiling water in long strips.

Cook the Spätzle (pasta) until they float to the top.

When they are done, drain and put into a buttered casserole dish with layers of cheese. Finish up with onions.

Bake in the oven for 20 minutes at 200°c.

You'll find Spätzle on the menu in Southern Germany. Done in the oven with Emmental cheese and onions it is quite a rich meal and best eaten with a plate of green salad.

White-rumped vulture

In January 2006 Markus Handschuh from Germany and Isadora Martinez from Colombia took joint managerial responsibility for Angkor Centre for Conservation of Biodiversity, Cambodia's first nature conservation centre, situated near the famous temples of Angkor Wat. Markus is in charge of a programme that aims to rescue, breed and re-introduce some highly endangered animals into the wild.

Markus Handschuh

At the entrance to the centre the visitor is greeted by a huge painting of feasting vultures. Three Asian vultures are depicted, the red-headed *Sarcogyps calvus* [CR]; the white-rumped *Gyps bengalensis* [CR] and the slender-billed vulture *Gyps tenuirostris* [CR].

Bean Stew | Uganda
Bijanjaalo na lumonde

Serves 4

- 250g red beans or use kidney beans
- 500g sweet potatoes
- oil
- 1 onion
- 3 tomatoes
- salt and pepper

How to make:

Soak the beans in water the night before. Cook next day for one hour.

Peel and cut up the sweet potato and add to the cooked beans. Simmer for another 30 minutes.

Dice the onion and fry gently. Add the cut-up tomatoes and season with salt and pepper.

Cook for 10 minutes over a low flame, then pour the tomato sauce over the beans.

Serve with ugali* or rice.

* Ugali is the most popular staple in Uganda. Sprinkle 3 cups maizemeal into 4 cups boiling water, whilst stirring continuously until it thickens, then simmer for 5-10 minutes until it is quite firm and solid. Turn over in the pot a few times and serve.

Mountain gorilla

David Baluku, after 7 years of working with Uganda Wildlife Education Centre in Entebbe, became the co-founder and project coordinator of DORDWEEP, a community project in Kasese district. Its motto is: "Man and Earth I care - do you?" The aim is to make a connection between community development and the conservation of wildlife.

David Baluku

As an offshoot from DORDWEEP, a new company was created: Kifaru African Expeditions. It promises to take you, the visitor, not only on exciting safari trips but also on guided tours to see mountain gorillas in the wild. Proceeds from it go directly to local communities and schools around protected areas in Kasese District. David himself often takes visitors to watch mountain gorillas *Gorilla beringei* [EN] and other animals in the wild.

Brocco Bella Lasagne | Canada

Serves 4

- 800g chopped tomatoes
- a sprinkle of oregano, basil and parsley
- tabasco sauce (optional)
- salt and pepper
- 6 sheets of lasagne
- 200g of spinach
- 125g crème fraiche
- 125g feta cheese, cubed
- 2-3 heads broccoli
- 60g grated mozzarella

How to make:

Cook the tomatoes with herbs, Tabasco (if using), salt and pepper to make a sauce on a low heat for approx. 30 minutes. Thoroughly wash the broccoli and chop into little pieces. Steam or boil till tender. Wash the spinach.

Mix the cubed feta cheese with the Creme Fraiche.

In a rectangular dish (20cm x 22cm) build up layers as follows: thin layer of sauce, lasagne sheets, ½ of broccoli, sauce, pasta, ½ spinach, feta with crème fraiche, sauce, lasagne sheets, rest of spinach, feta with crème fraiche, broccoli, sauce, lasagne sheets, thin layer of sauce. Cover with tin foil and bake for 25-30 minutes at 200°C.

Remove foil, cover with a layer of mozzarella cheese, and put back in the oven for 5 minutes. Remove from the oven and enjoy!

This recipe is a testimony to creative vegetarians the world over. They can conjure up a tantalisingly tasty meal from whatever they find in the kitchen cupboard, then give it a fancy name and invite their friends round.

Natasha behind the scenes with a Ring-tailed coati at Durrell wildlife park

Natasha Lloyd is working at the Centre for Conservation Research at Calgary Zoo. She is studying the population density and distribution of the black-tailed prairie dog *Cynomys ludovicianus* [LC] in Canada.

Her research will help with the planned re-introduction of another animal, the black-footed ferret *Mustela nigripes* [EN], which is a predator of the black-tailed prairie dog. To find out the chances of this ferret surviving in the wild, one must find out whether there is a big enough food supply, i.e. enough prairie dogs.

Ring-tailed coati *Nasua nasua* [LC]

Black-tailed prairie dog

Cornmeal Coo Coo | Trinidad

Serves 4

- 190g of cornmeal
- 350-400ml water
- 12 okras
- salt and black pepper to taste
- 1 can of coconut milk

How to make:

Slice the okras, boil in coconut milk until soft.

Stir enough water into the cornmeal to make a paste, and add to the okras. Cook on a low heat whilst stirring until it forms a stiff ball.

When the coo coo is stiff and can hold a peak, pour into a buttered bowl and shake busily around, it will form a ball (panada) which you can slice.

If you like, you can press down the slices with the back of a spoon and add a little butter.

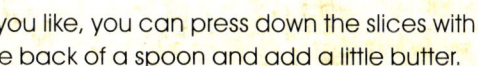

This recipe is excellent with fish and a salad.

West Indian manatee (VU)

Risha Alleyne is working to safeguard Environmentally Sensitive Species and Areas (ESSA) within Trinidad and Tobago. This can mean anything from drafting local legislation for reserves, to developing educational materials for schools, to improving public awareness. Thanks to the work of her department there are now three nature reserves in Trinidad and Tobago. Nariva Swamp is one of these.

It is home to 58 species of mammal, 37 species of reptile, and 171 species of birds, unfortunately also home to 92 species of mosquito! Some of the more interesting animals that can be seen here, are howler monkeys *Alouatta* [VU]; capuchin monkeys *Cebus* [LC]; anacondas *Eunectes* [LC]; caimans *Caiman crocodilus* [LC] and the vulnerable West Indian manatee *Trichechus manatus* [VU].

Risha Alleyne

Sweet

Rice Pudding | India
Kheer

Serves 4

- 150g shortgrain rice
- 240ml water
- 1 litre milk
- 370ml evaporated milk
- 8 tbsp. sugar
- 5 crushed green cardamoms
- few strands of saffron
- 10 blanched almonds
- handful of raisins

How to make:

Wash the rice and soak in water for half an hour. Boil the rice in the same water with the addition of milk and simmer on low heat for 15-20 minutes. Add saffron strands. Scrape out the mixture sticking to the sides and the bottom of the pan and mash the rice while stirring frequently.

Gradually add evaporated milk to the above mixture. When it is of creamy consistency, add sugar and stir until dissolved.

Cook the rice till it becomes thick and creamy again.

Remove from the heat; add crushed green cardamom seeds and the blanched almonds and raisins. Serve hot or cold.

When milk is slowly condensed with rice, the result is a rich creamy dessert. No need to add evaporated milk is my personal opinion. Very little rice goes a long way, 50g will do for 2 litres milk.

Shikha with Maggie Esson -
Durrell Education Department

Shikha Nalin from India regularly spoils her family and friends with her good Indian cooking. For twelve years she worked in the Education Department at Delhi Zoo. In 2003 she took part in the Durrell Endangered Species Management Graduate Certificate Course in Jersey, where her project 'Evaluation in Education' attracted the attention of staff there.

Rock python
Python sebae [LC].

Shikha with a rock
python at Durrell

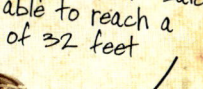

Rock pythons are said
to be able to reach a
length of 32 feet

Sweet Potato Pudding | Cuba
Boniatillo

Serves 4

- 240ml water
- 1 cinnamon stick
- lemon peel
- 200g light brown sugar
- 2-3 sweet potatoes
- 1 tsp. salt
- 2 tbsp. cornflour
- 3 tbsp. cream
- 1 tbsp. cinnamon sugar (optional)
- handful of roast peanuts (optional)

How to make:

Put 2 cups of water into a saucepan and simmer with the cinnamon stick and lemon peel for about 20 mins, or until the water is reduced to half. Drain off the liquid and keep.

Peel the sweet potatoes and cook in water with a teaspoonful of salt, until they are soft. Drain and mash the sweet potatoes to a purée.

Take the liquid reserved from the first step and add the brown sugar. Bring to the boil.

Add the purée to the mixture and cook for another 5 minutes. Stir 3 tablespoons of cream into 2 tablespoons of cornflour, and use this to thicken the purée. Fill into bowls and leave to cool.

To make this dish more festive, sprinkle some cinnamon sugar on top, add crushed roasted peanuts and some thin strips of orange peel.

Alicia sets up a trap to catch voles to measure their population size whilst in Jersey

Alicia Perez Angel is doing research particularly on small animals which are endemic to Cuba. The Cuban solenodon *Solenodon cubanas* [EN] was once thought to be extinct. It has the appearance of an oversize rat. It is a nocturnal animal living in the dense rainforest in the South East of Cuba. Solenodons are almost blind, relying on their sense of touch and smell. What is special about the Cuban solenodon? Apart from being Gerald Durrell's favourite animal, they hunt by stunning their prey with their venomous bite. They don't harm people, and because they feed on insects, they might be rather useful for keeping down pests.

Cuban solenodon

Spiced Honey Cake | Israel
Lekach

Makes
2 loaves

- 280g plain flour
- 2 tsp baking powder
- 2 tsp bicarbonate of soda
- 1 tsp cinnamon
- 1 tsp allspice
- 1/2 tsp salt
- 4 tsp instant coffee in 100ml boiling water
- 130g soft brown sugar
- 300g runny honey
- 200ml sunflower oil
- 2 eggs

How to make:

Sift the flour with the baking powder, bicarbonate of soda, cinnamon, allspice and salt into a large mixing bowl.

Make a cup of strong coffee.

In a separate bowl, combine the beaten eggs with the sugar, honey and oil. Then add the coffee and the dry ingredients, stirring to prevent clumping. It should be of pouring consistency.

Grease 2 loaf pans, or line with greaseproof paper, then pour the mixture in. Bake at 180°C for 25 - 30 minutes. When ready, the cake should feel firm, but springy.

Leave to cool in the tins for 5 minutes, then turn out onto a wire rack.

This cake rises A LOT so if its too high in the pan (more than half way), it will spill over.

If you want to make it look a bit special, you can decorate the top with almonds, walnuts or apple slices.

The picture shows crowned cranes in Jerusalem Biblical Zoo

Na'ama Ben-David

Na'ama Ben-David, now living in the US, used to work in the Jerusalem Biblical Zoo in Israel. This zoo is an oasis in an otherwise war-torn country, and a great facility for schools and for families. Na'ama is now involved with a number of projects, between the Biblical Zoo in Jerusalem, the Nashville Zoo in Tennessee (USA) and her own non-profit foundation called Suluhisha, which deals with sustainable economic development and HIV/AIDS education for women in sub-Saharan Africa.

Crowned crane *Balearica regulorum* [VU].

Banana Bread | Cameroon

Makes
1 loaf

- 4 ripe bananas (or plantains)
- 250g plain flour
- 1 tsp. baking powder
- 1 tsp. bicarbonate of soda
- 125g butter or margarine
- 125g soft brown sugar
- 1 tbsp Demerara sugar
- 2 eggs, beaten

How to make:

Mash 3 bananas. In a big bowl combine all dry ingredients.

In another bowl beat together first butter and sugar, then add the eggs and the mashed banana. Gradually add the flour mixture by the spoonful, stirring all the time.

Put into a greased 2lb loaf tin. It should be about $2/3$ full. Decorate the top with slices of banana and give it a dusting of brown sugar.

Bake in the oven at 180°C for 1¼ hour.

When you have taken it out of the oven, leave it in the tin for another 15 mins, then turn out on a wire rack. Leave to cool.

Here are three ways to improve this cake:

Sift the flour to begin with, add a teaspoon of cinnamon to the flour, mix 2 teaspoons of lemon juice into the mashed banana.

David measures tree distances with a laser finder

Between May and August 2007 David Lekeaka from Cameroon spent many hours looking up at nests of chimpanzees *Pan troglodytes* [EN] in the trees and taking measurements. He was comparing nesting height and diameter of nesting area in two separate populations of chimpanzees, to see whether proximity with human activity had an effect on nesting habits. He found that it did. With denser human settlements or hunters' paths nearby, the chimpanzees tended to build their nests higher up and spread their nests over a bigger area.

As the apes come into conflict with people in competition for the forest's resources, solutions have to be found which actively involve local people in conservation without threatening their livelihood.

Apricot Tart | France
Tart aux Abricots

Serves 4

- 200g plain flour
- 1 egg
- 50g melted butter
- 3 tbsp. sunflower oil
- pinch of salt
- 150g sugar
- 75g butter
- 75g plain flour
- 50g ground almonds
- 2 tsp. vanilla sugar
- 500g apricots

How to make:

Prepare the pastry: Mix the first five ingredients. Make into a ball and leave to stand in a cool place for 1 hour.

Prepare the filling: With your fingertips mix the butter, sugar, vanilla sugar, ground almond and flour.

Roll out the pastry to fit into your flan tin, so that the pastry comes up on the sides. Now cut the apricots in half and spread over the pastry. Cover with the filling. Put in the oven at 180°C for 40 minutes.

Enjoy warm or cold.

Whatever the fruit in season, you can probably make a tart with it. Plums and cherries are great favourites. Serve with cream, vanilla ice cream, or créme anglaise.

Snacks

Cheese Bread | Brazil
Pão de Queijo

Serves 4

- ½ glass of soy oil (120ml) (or any vegetable oil)
- 1 glass of milk (240ml)
- 3 eggs
- 250g white cheese, grated*
- 1.2 kg manioc or tapioca flour
- ½ kg of manioc flour
- 1 dessert spoon of salt

How to make:

Put the manioc flour in a bowl. Mix oil, milk and salt together and bring to the boil. As soon as it boils, turn off the flame and gradually add to the manioc flour – mix well.

Add the eggs, one by one, and stir until the dough becomes soft. Add the cheese and mix with the dough until it no longer sticks to your hands.

Make small balls and put on a baking tray, spaced slightly apart.

Put the tray in a pre-heated oven at 200°C, for 30 minutes.

Take out the bread as soon as it becomes golden brown.

* White cheese is a mature cheese from the South of Brazil, made from cow's milk, it is yellowish with a white core, punctuated with lots of tiny bubbles of air. Substitute with havarti, gruyere or cheddar.

Fernando with a sedated jaguar, *Panthera onca* (NT) in order to monitor its health

Fernando Lima from Brazil studied biology at the university of Minas Gerais before attending the 2006 Durrell Endangered Species Management Graduate Certificate Course in Jersey, where he would write his project 'The Leap of the Cat' to prepare him for the next step into the wild. Now he is busy tracking ocelots and collecting data between the rivers Parana and Paranapanema in the South of Brazil, an area the size of Wales, with pockets of land where these elegant felines still roam freely.

Potato and Carrot Tart | Latvia
Sklaudu Rausi

Pastry:
Serves 4
- 2 glasses (450g) of rye flour* + 2 tbsp. soft butter + ½ glass water (120ml) + salt.

Filling:
- 3 large mashed potatos
- 2 large mashed cooked carrots
- 2 tbsp. butter or double cream
- 1 egg yolk
- 1 egg
- ½ tsp. caraway seeds
- salt

How to make:

Prepare the pastry – Work ingredients into a firm pastry, leave to rest for a while. Roll out and cut rounds of 15cm diameter. Press into muffin tins so that the edges come up 1-2cm on the sides.

Prepare the filling – to the mashed potato add butter, egg yolk and caraway seeds. To the carrots add butter or cream, and one egg. Mix both well, but keep them separate.

Put a thin layer of potato into the patties, top with the carrot mash. Bake for 15 mins at 180°, until the pastry is cooked and the top is bright orange.

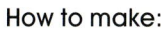

* Rye flour is commonly used for bread baking in Germany and Eastern Europe, it is lower in gluten and higher in fibre than wheat flour. If you are not near a Polish or German shop, try your local wholefood store.

Ilze at Riga Zoo monitoring exotic species

Ilze Dunce from Latvia is the Head of the Amphibian department at Riga Zoo, monitoring local and exotic species, while organising educational activities for the public. She is also in charge of the breeding programmes for amphibians at the zoo. These include the tree Frog *Hyla arborea* [LC] and the mossy frog *Theloderma corticale* [DD].

The tree frog is commonly found in many parts of Europe. It can be used as a model to study other frogs. The mossy frog is endangered and requires careful handling.

Tree frog

Potato Croquettes | Sumatra
Pergedel Kentang

Serves 4
Makes 12 croquettes

- 5 potatoes approximately 150g in weight
- the leafy part of celery (or a bunch green of spring onions)
- pepper and salt
- 1 onion - finely diced
- 1-2 eggs
- oil

How to make:

Boil and mash the potatoes, then season with salt and pepper.

Slice the celery or spring onion very thinly.

Cut and fry the onion until brown.

Mix all together into a stiff paste. When it has cooled down a bit, form this mass into small balls with your hands, the size of a golf ball. Before frying them, they have to be covered in beaten egg.

Fry in deep oil and turn regularly. They are ready when golden brown.

A similar snack is Pergedel Jagung, which is made with rice flour and fresh corn. Grind the fresh corn until soupy, then mix with rice flour, minced celery or spring onion, a bit of garlic, salt and pepper. Shape and fry like Pergedel Kentang.

Elva tiger-tracking

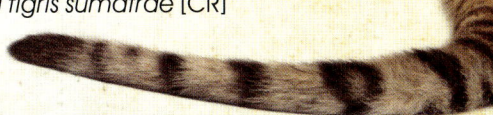

Elva Gemita from Sumatra worked as a research assistant for the Tiger Project in Jambi, Northern Sumatra, using radio-tracking equipment to find the tigers and monitor their movements. In a landscape largely made up of oil palm plantations and forested areas, conservationists, in cooperation with plantation owners, are trying to create 'wildlife corridors' which will allow individuals to move between one group of tigers and another, without posing too much of a threat to the people who live and work in the plantations.

Sumatran tiger *Panthera tigris sumatrae* [CR]

Chapatti | India
Chapatti

Makes 6 chapattis:

- 150ml water
- 500g chapatti flour
- pinch of salt
- knob of butter to taste

How to make:

Slowly pour the water into the flour, just enough to knead into a soft pliable dough. This may take 8 minutes. Leave covered for 1-2 hours. Knead again (1min), and form into 6 balls. Cover.

Heat up a non-stick pan or griddle to medium heat. Dust each ball with flour and roll out into an even thin disk. Slap between your hands to get rid of any excess flour and cook on a hot plate until bubbles appear on the upper side.

Turn over and cook briefly until spots appear on the underside. If you have gas, hold the chapatti over it with a pair of tongs, to make it puff up, then stack the chapattis on a plate and keep them warm under a clean cloth.

In India people eat chapattis with most meals. They are particularly good with curries and dals. Best eaten fresh and with a knob of butter melted into each chapatti.

Sat Pal and his survey team

Sat Pal Dhiman from Northern India is working as a range officer in Himachal Pradesh. He is responsible for protecting wildlife in two reserves. One of them, Majathal, provides the ideal habitat for the cheer pheasant *Catreus wallichii* [VU]. This bird, once a favourite game bird, has become quite rare in the hills of Himachal Pradesh, with only a few small and isolated populations left.

To safeguard their survival, a breeding programme has been developed. Breeding cheer pheasant is part of Sat Pal's work for conservation.

Chapatti Wrap | Uganda
Rolex

Serves 4

- 4 big chapattis (to make your own see page 12, or you buy ready-made)
- 6 eggs
- 1 onion
- 2 tomatoes
- cabbage or cos lettuce
- salt and pepper

How to make:

Cut up half of the onion and one tomato into very small pieces and mix with beaten egg. Season.

Take one chapatti and drag it through this eggy mixture.

Fry on both sides. Repeat with the rest of the chapattis.

Finally top with shredded crunchy cabbage or salad and a few slices of tomato.

Roll up and serve as soon they are ready.

Usually called 'Rolex', these are popular after-school snacks sold at wayside stalls.

Poachers handing over their illegal hunting implements

Simon Akwetaireho from Uganda has been working with the Rwenzori Mountains National Park as a community conservation warden. For the people, who live around the park, the forests are a source of building materials, fuel wood, medicines, honey, animal products, and other resources.

His work involves the delicate task of laying down the law on poaching, while at the same time educating local people how they can harvest the forest sustainably.

The picture shows poachers handing over their illegal hunting implements as a result of talks and meetings with the Park Authorities.

Spicy Potatoes | India
Til Aloo Dum

Serves 4

- 400g potatoes
- 2 tbsp. oil
- 1 tsp. cumin seeds
- ½ tsp. turmeric
- ½ tsp. red chili powder (according to taste)
- salt to taste
- 10g sesame seeds

How to make:

Dry roast the sesame seeds in a pan, grind coarsely and set aside.

Boil the potatoes until they are just done. Peel the boiled potatoes and cut into quarters if the potatoes are big, and into halves if the potatoes are small.

Gently heat the oil, adding a quarter of a teaspoon of turmeric powder, half a teaspoon of red chili powder and salt to taste, then add the pieces of potatoes taking care not to splash. Stir fry until the potatoes are slightly brown.

Before serving, sprinkle the coarsely ground sesame seeds over the potatoes.

Together with hot puris this makes a filling snack. Puris are made from balls of dough like chapattis, a bit smaller in size. They are then flattened and deep fried until they puff up.

Sunita presenting silver plate and scarf
to Lee Durrell - a symbol of goodwill

Sunita Pradhan from India works as a scientific officer at Padmaja Naidu Himalayan Zoological Park, in the province of Darjeeling. This high altitude zoo specialises in breeding rare animals from the Himalayas such as the red panda *Ailurus fulgens* [VU] and the snow leopard *Panthera unica* [EN].

In a recent success story, four red pandas have been reintroduced back into their wild habitat.

Red panda - Central Asia

Snow leopard - Central Asia

Seven year old orangutan in Sumatra

Valerie Marchal from France came to Jersey in 2003 and 2004 to study Durrell's marmosets and orangutans. She went on to complete her Masters in Primate Conservation, by studying the conflicts that exist between humans and primates in Indonesia. In the course of her research she visited four villages in Northern Sumatra, talking with local people about their fear of primates raiding their crops.

Sumatran orangutan *Pongo abelii* [CR]

Valerie with a translator, interviewing a farmer.

Glossary

achuete juice in Filipino cooking is the liquid made by soaking annato seeds in water. Its purpose is to colour food red, its taste can be described as slightly sweet and peppery.

bagoong is a fish paste made from fermented shrimp and fish. If you can't find bagoong in your local Asian shop, use fish sauce or anchovy paste instead.

banana bud, a dark maroon-leaved blossom or bud growing in the middle of a bunch of bananas, only available canned in the UK.

bok choy is part of the brassica family, similar in taste to Chinese cabbage, but more loose-leaved, with dark green leaves and thick white ribs, can be grown in the UK.

caraway seeds, brown curved seeds, similar to cumin seeds, but with their own distinctive flavour, commonly used in rye bread, cakes and cheeses in Central and Eastern Europe.

cardamoms, aromatic seeds held in a green pod, added to rice pudding, cakes and curries.

cassava/manioc, a root with a fine dark skin, very starchy, it is used to make a fine flour. It must be boiled when eaten whole, as it contains toxins. Cassava is grown in South America, Africa and Asia. The flour is available in the UK.

chapatti flour, a low-gluten wholemeal flour, that can be made into a very soft and pliable dough, it may be substituted with half white and half wholemeal flour. Try Indian and Asian shops.

rice wine is an alcoholic beverage made from rice. It is clear, beige or reddish brown in colour and has an alcoholic content of 15-25%. Popular in different varieties in many Asian countries, it is made by fermenting rice starch into sugars, which convert into alcohol. Available in Chinese or Asian shops.

cilantro, fresh green coriander leaves, as common in Asia as parsley is in Europe, available from greengrocers. Can be grown in the UK.

crystallized sugar, sugar made into large crystals, clear, brown and yellow in colour, it is used in Chinese savoury dishes for its subtle, mellow flavour and to give a translucent finish to roasted dishes. Chinese and Asian shops.

cumin powder is made from cumin seeds, usually part of a mixture of spices used in curries.

cumin seeds yellowish-brown moon-crescent shaped seeds, similar to caraway seeds, they add a warm aromatic flavour to dishes.

fish sauce is a brown sauce with a pungent aroma, made from salting and fermenting fish, often anchovies. It is commonly used in Southeast Asia as a condiment instead of salt or soy sauce. Available from Asian shops.

garam masala is a mixture of roasted and ground spices used in Indian cuisine, including warm spices like cardamom, coriander, cinnamon, cloves, nutmeg and pepper. If you can't get it locally, you can make up your own mixture, or use mixed spice, which is sold in shops for baking cakes.

ginger, the tuberous underground roots of the ginger plant, can be minced or sliced and added to sweet or savoury dishes to give it zest and flavour. Powdered ginger can be used as a substitute, but it will be less aromatic and more peppery.

ginger juice is the strained liquid made by pouring hot water over slices of root ginger, as if making tea, and letting it brew for a while.

harina is a pre-cooked, finely ground maize flour, white in colour, produced in Colombia and Venezuela, suitable for making arepas and empenadas. The PAN harina is usually available where there is a Portuguese or Spanish population. Not to be confused with polenta or maizemeal.

Irish potatoes are simply potatoes. In Uganda and Tanzania people distinguish between Irish potatoes and sweet potatoes; both are regarded as a vegetable usually served with rice.

manioc flour see cassava.

okras are green, ridged and pointed seed pods, which produce a sticky substance when cooked. You can buy them at some greengrocers, supplying Asian or Caribbean communities. Choose small firm okras.

plantains are members of the banana family, green or yellow, inedible raw, but wonderful baked, roasted, fried, or cooked. Peel by slitting the skin lengthways and removing the strips. Sometimes available at greengrocers.

rice flour is finely ground rice, often used to thicken stews. Available from wholefood shops. Substitute with cornflour.

rye flour, made from rye grain, is used for bread baking in Germany and Eastern Europe; it is lower in gluten and higher in fibre than wheat flour. If you are not near a Polish or German shop, try your local wholefood store.

sauerkraut is fermented white cabbage with a distinctive sour flavour. It is sold, usually in jars, at supermarkets and grocery shops.

turmeric like ginger is an underground rhizome, though rarely seen as a root in Europe. The bright yellow turmeric powder is widely available and is used mostly in curries.

vanilla sugar is made by adding extract from the vanilla bean to sugar. You can make it yourself by sticking one or two black vanilla pods into a jar of caster sugar and letting it infuse over time. Vanilla sugar is available from the baking section in supermarkets.

white cheese is a mature cheese from the South of Brazil, made from cow's milk, it is yellowish with a white core, punctuated with lots of tiny bubbles of air. As it is not easily available in Europe, one must look for a substitute. Any strong cheese that is hard enough to cut, but soft enough to melt, like muenster, havarti, gruyere or cheddar, will do.

zebu meat, is meat from zebu - domestic cattle, originally from India, with humps on their back. It is now common in many countries with tropical climates. Substitute with beef.

Photographers

Gerald Durrell and his legacy

Gerald Durrell's passion for the natural world began at an early age, with his experiences growing up on the island of Corfu. As a young man, he travelled extensively and his many trips captured in his books and films highlighted not only the wonders of nature, but also the threats that were increasingly being placed on them. He believed that zoos could be much more than collections of animals for public entertainment; they could have a direct role in conservation through the captive breeding and release of species to the wild.

Conservation activities in the field started early on in the organisation's history with expeditions in the 1960's to find the volcano rabbits of Mexico and in the 1970's to India and to St. Lucia for our first field project on the endemic Amazon parrot.

Gerald then visited Mauritius and became fascinated by the beauty of the island but also alarmed by the loss of its native species. Work started on the restoration of the Mauritius kestrel and progressed to other iconic bird species and the restoration of Round Island. Soon after this, the organisation became involved in Madagascar, initially working to protect the critically endangered ploughshare tortoise.

To complement our world renowned animal husbandry and breeding skills, we have developed a range of expertise to conserve species in their natural habitats. We use a variety of scientific techniques to assess conservation problems and design and evaluate management solutions. We conduct hands-on management of endangered species populations, control the impacts of invasive species, and work with local communities to reduce pressures on species and habitats.

Gerald Durrell with a Telfair's skink

Durrell training in depth

Training

Our International Training Centre has been providing training in endangered species conservation techniques for over 20 years. Since its establishment in 1985 we have trained nearly 3,000 conservationists from over 128 countries. With a dedicated teaching facility and accommodation at the wildlife park, we have been able to bring conservationists from around the world to gain hands-on experience with animal management as well as more theoretical training in species conservation.

In the field

Our field programmes are based primarily in the most imperilled island ecosystems in the world. We currently manage 50 projects which are located in 14 countries and one third of the organisation's total staff are based overseas where they work closely with local authorities and NGO partners.

Always led by the need to restore species, our approaches vary in scale and response to suit the situation or the ground. In many cases, our involvement with a particular species has developed into a series of projects aimed at improving the underlying threats facing that species and its habitat.

Wildlife park

The wildlife park has been the cornerstone of Durrell as an institution since it opened as Jersey Zoo in 1959. As well as home to our animal collection, the park also serves as our headquarters and location for the International Training Centre. Our animal collection supports conservation through breeding programmes, the provision of skills and training to conservationists and as an important tool for communicating with the general public.